CHRISTMAS IN GERMANY

TABLE OF CONTENTS

Published By
World Book Encyclopedia, Inc.
Chicago, Illinois

Staff for this Book

Editor
Peter Andrews

Art Director
Don Menell

Associate Editors
Anje Berger
Gene Gleason

Assistant Editor
Constance Segur

Graphics Researcher
Yvonne Freund

INTRODUCTION

There is a special magic about Christmas in Germany that transcends its borders. No other country has shared more of its Christmas tradition with the rest of the world. From the brightly illuminated tree to Saint Nicholas, himself, the German Christmas heritage is now universal. The luxurious Christmas celebration seen on these pages is a re-creation from the classic German novel, *Buddenbrooks*, by

Nobel Prize winning Thomas Mann. This, of course, is only one kind of German celebration. Those "Christmas Keeping Germans," as one historian called them, are just as joyous in an apartment or even in a barn. Christmas is kept in the heart.

In this book, the first in a series designed to explore the magic of Christmas all over the world, you will trace the growth of Christmas

in Germany. In the accompanying package you will find a German Christmas angel. Similar to the angels sold at the *Christkindlmarkts* throughout Germany, they were first created by a German father grieving the death of his only daughter more than 300 years ago.

You will also find recipe cards to help you bring some of the delights of a German Christmas Feast into your own home, making them part of the Christmas memories your children will carry on in years to come.

Christmas in Germany is more than just a holiday. It's an entire season devoted to merry making and deep religious devotion to the Christ Child.

Preparations begin long before the actual season starts. For weeks the air is filled with the tingly smell of ginger and cinnamon. And as the day itself draws nearer, shop windows fairly burst with all sorts of Christmas toys and delights.

With this book you will also find an Advent Calendar to help you count off the days until Christmas. Similar to the calendars German children have opened day by day for centuries as Christmas approaches, it is yet another way to help bring German Christmas traditions into your home.

We hope that this book will help make this Christmas season a little different and a little brighter for you and your family. And that in years to come, as you collect these books, your family will include traditions from around the world in your Christmas festivities.

We wish you all a *"Fröliche Weinachten."*

THE EDITORS

A CHRISTMAS GIFT TO THE WORLD

Whether they are seeking the exaltation of the spirit or enjoyment of physical man, the Germans seem to get more enjoyment out of Christmas than almost any other people on earth. The German Christmas celebration lasts a full month and a half, from the end of November to mid-January. This festival season is illuminated by joyous carols, colorful fairs, deep devotion to the Christ Child, playful recreations of hellish demons and a parade of seasonal foods and Christmas candies that turns the most dedicated dieter into a bloated *Naschkatze*—snack snatcher.

It isn't enough for a German to have fun during the Christmas season. He insists that everyone share in the joy of the holiday season. Much of Germany is transformed into a vast nationwide block party. Homes are thrown open to friends, relatives and even casual neighbors who come in and out to exchange presents, look at the tree and wish each other well over a glass of punch. Children are loaded down with cookies and gingerbread creations, which are almost always bad for them, but this time mother doesn't complain. After all, she has been baking some of them since July. Young men dress up in outlandish costumes to look like fearsome spirits and scare little children into being good. The children are only too glad to go along because in Germany, even a hobgoblin may have a spare present for a deserving youngster.

No one is left out. Household pets and even farm animals can expect to receive a gaily wrapped Christmas present or a special treat from their owners.

In virtually every German village, city and town there is a *Christkindlmarkt* — Christ Child Market—with brightly lit booths selling fruits, candies, sausages, cookies and toys. Usually these fairs take place in the town square or in front of the largest church. Automobiles are barred from the market area and children can roam among the stalls to their hearts' content—staring, buying, hoping and, perhaps, dropping a none too subtle hint to their parents about something that particularly catches their eye.

The meanest grump, sulking in his solitary attic, can scarcely escape the cheerful clamor of church bells or the music of street carolers. From the lilting melodies sung by the choirs in the cathedrals of Nuremberg to the thunder of New Year's Eve shotgun fire rattling through the mountains of Berchtesgaden, the whole country is alive with the sounds of Christmas.

The German people—and here we are talking about the centuries old culture of northern and central Europe rather than the present political creation—have had such an abundance of the Christmas spirit that they gave some of it to the rest of the world. The Christmas tree, now an almost universal symbol of the season, is clearly a German creation. The lights and bright ornaments we put on the tree are also gifts to the world from Germany. The gingerbread house, which looks too good to eat but isn't, is a part of the German yuletide tradition. So also are such carols as *Silent Night* and *O Tannenbaum*. Saint Nicholas, much changed from his original folklore origin, is a happy immigrant from Germany.

But for most of us, the most enduring part of the German Christmas heritage is the tree itself. One legend links the birth of the Christmas tree with Saint Boniface an English monk who organized the Christian church in France and Germany during the middle years of the Eighth Century. One Christmas Eve, somewhere in the forests of northern Germany, the missionary came upon a group of worshipers who had gathered around an oak tree to sacrifice the son of their chief, little child Prince Asulf, to the god Thor. Saint Boniface clearly

"...ALL THE ANIMALS BEGAN TO TALK"

An early woodcut depicts the December 6th journey of St. Nicholas through the countryside.

opposed the execution and according to various legends either flattened the mighty oak with one blow of his fist, ordered it chopped down or whacked it with an ax and the wind toppled it. However he managed it, the oak went down and a small fir tree sprang up instantly in its place. Saint Boniface told the awed spectators that this was the Tree of Life, representing Christ.

A Tenth Century legend holds that when Christ was born, all the forest animals began to talk and, despite the darkness and deep snow, every tree blossomed and bore fruit. All the trees paid homage to the newborn King, with the embarrassed exception of a tiny fir tree from the North who was so insignificant in stature and appearance that the other trees tried to hide her. She had just about mustered a deep-green blush when the Lord intervened —stars fell from Heaven, lighted on the fir's branches and illuminated them like a sparkling diamond necklace.

Another German fir tree legend is that a poor forester welcomed a strange child into his cottage one snowy Christmas Eve, feeding him and putting him up for the night. Next morning the befriended youngster, who was actually the Christ Child, caused a small, glittering fir tree to grow beside the forester's door. The happy host took it inside to become the first Christmas tree.

Martin Luther is the hero of still another Christmas tree legend. One Christmas Eve, while strolling through a snow-covered forest, he was deeply affected by the beauty of the starlight gleaming on the branches of the evergreens. He cut down a small fir tree, took it into his home and placed lighted candles on its boughs so that his wife and children might behold the same heavenly light that had dazzled him. Luther did not mention the incident in his writings, but the legend grew and as a result the strongly Roman Catholic southern portions of Germany resisted using a tree as part of their Christmas observance until about a century ago. Some authorities believe that the Christmas tree made its way to southern Germany by way of America. If that's true, it is fair enough. For the Christmas tree was first brought to the colonies by Hessian soldiers during the American Revolution. Whatever its travels, the Christmas tree is now popular throughout Germany.

The tree, as we know it today, began in the early Middle Ages. Germany, then Catholic, observed Christmas with a religious play presented in village squares or in front of churches. Variously called a Paradise play, Mystery or Miracle play, it dramatized the Creation and Fall of Man with the promise of Christ's return. It was presented with only

Children playing with a special Christmas toy, an elaborately carved nutcracker.

one stage "prop"—the *Paradeisbaum* (Paradise Tree)—a fir tree with apples hung on its branches. These plays became irreverent and were banned by the church, but the Paradise Tree lived on in the homes of the faithful. Householders decorated them with small white wafers, symbolic of the Holy Eucharist. These, in turn, gave way to bits of pastry, cookies and cakes; each of them cut to represent some figure or event of the Nativity.

Until the 16th Century, the Christmas tree had a serious rival—the Pyramid—a tripod or pyramidal set of shelves arranged one above the other. Candles were set along the shelf edges and the shelves were filled with small gifts and fruit. Often a crib for the Christ Child was placed at the foot of the Pyramid. Eventually people began to transfer the lights and the crib to the tree itself.

Brilliantly decorated and sparkling with lights, the German Christmas tree proceeded to win the world's favor. Prince Albert of Saxony, the husband of England's Queen Victoria, had a tree set up at Windsor Castle in 1841, launching a fashion that spread quickly throughout all of England.

Despite the predominantly happy character of a German Christmas, there are enough villains, demons and spoilsports hovering over the holiday to scare the wits out of a suggestible young child.

Suppose you are a little boy or girl living in Germany, desperately hoping that Saint Nicholas will bring you a gift on Christmas Eve. In the first place you learn that Saint Nick has no reindeer. That's just a silly modern idea cooked up by the Americans or someone else. In the second place even if he did, that is no guarantee he would be bringing you anything you wanted. The German Saint Nicholas is not an eternally jolly fellow like our Santa Claus. Although he is the patron saint of children, he can be a stern figure. Most German legends picture him riding over the countryside on a white pony with two bags. One filled with presents if you have been good and one filled with switches if you have been bad—and *he knows*.

In older days things were easier. Odin, the old Norse Boss of Everything, had an eight-footed horse named Sleipnir that he used to ride through the forests in mid-winter, delivering only presents to people. And that Thor, the Chief Executive of Thunder, drove through the heavens like a celestial hot rodder in his golden chariot drawn by two white goats, Cracker and Gnasher. He too was widely known for his lavish hand with gifts. And there was Frau Bertha, also called Hertha, goddess of hearth and home, who could be very generous when she wanted to be.

But all this means little to you, a child of today. These worthy benefactors have long since given up active practice. They don't make house calls any more.

And what have you to replace them? A line-up of villains that would frighten the strongest

"...GERMANS INSIST EVERYONE SHARE IN THE JOY OF THE SEASON"

Germans customarily give presents to all the children on Christmas Eve.

youngster — *Hans Muff, Knecht Rupprecht, Butz, Hans Tripp, Krampus, Klaubauf, Bartel, Perchta, Buzebergt, Budelfrau, 12 Buttenmandln, Pelznickel,* the *Berchtenrunner Mob* and the notorious *Habersack.* Each of them has a face that would disgrace a wanted poster.

Some may bring you presents, although you might not like the way they are delivered. Some bring you a present of a lump of coal. Some don't bring presents at all. They take them.

"BY THE TIME
YOU GET IT UNWRAPPED,
CHRISTMAS
IS OUT OF SEASON"

*Along with the gifts for good children comes
the villain to punish the not so very good.*

Krampus has a long tail, a red, snake-like tongue and he carries a basket on his back. This basket is where you may wind up on Christmas Eve, if he thinks you deserve it.

What about this *Knecht Rupprecht?* He uses a couple of aliases—*Pelznickel* and *Servant Ruppert*—depending on what part of the country he is in. Sometimes he has a floor-length beard and a fur coat that's eight sizes too big. He's supposed to be Saint Nick's helper. If he gives you a bad report, there will be no presents from Saint Nicholas—maybe a switch or perhaps a lump of coal.

The *Berchtenrunner Mob* have you out numbered from the start. They come around to your farm in horrible masks and remind you how much their Queen Bee, *Frau Bertha,* has done for your crops. And what have you done for her lately, they ask while rattling their chains and making wild swings with their pick-axes. No gifts from *them;* they expect you to give them something. Better cough up or forget about Christmas.

How do you cope, for example, with a Christmas spook who is not only invisible but has no name? In spite of these natural limitations, he's a household no-name in northern Germany. He slips up to your house on Christmas Eve, flings open the front door, throws in a gift and is out of sight before you've recovered your wits. This odd spirit is called *Julkapp* or *Klopfelscheit,* but that's no help. Besides Mr. Anonymous always wraps up the gift like a Chinese puzzle. By the time you get it unwrapped, Christmas is out of season.

For many Germans, however, Christmas never seems to be out of season. As early as the previous July, the hard-working *hausfrau* has begun baking honey and almond cookies called *Lebkuchen* and gingerbread known as *Pfefferkuchen* that will stay fresh until Christmas. Unless they are watched carefully, however, the chances are that these early entries, even when supplemented by hundreds of later morsels such as *Springerle,* little hard cakes with designs on top, will disappear long before.

The German Christmas season itself extends from Saint Andrew's Night (November 30) to the Octave of Epiphany (January 13). In that 45-day span there are 18-calorie-crowded holidays or festivals plus enough subordinate celebrations to wipe out any unwanted intervals of rest. Only the most con-

Today St. Nick is still followed by villains as he makes his rounds checking on the children.

firmed Christmas keeper could hope to make all the stops on this Christmas itinerary. But quite a few of them try.

November 30—Saint Andrew's Night—On this night young girls are supposed to have a dream which will predict the identity of their future husbands. Actually, Saint Andrew is the patron saint of Scotland, but many Germans include it in their Christmas season to get started a day early.

December 1 — First Sunday of Advent — The Advent season lasts until Christmas with a new Advent candle being lighted each week. Children open a new window of their cardboard Advent Calendar each day until Christmas and recite a prayer for the day.

A brightly decorated Marzipan soldier is designed to hang from the Christmas tree.

December 4—Saint Barbara's Day—Early-budding cherry branches are cut and put in water beside the stove so they'll bloom by Christmas. The Nuremberg Fair, *Christkindl-markt,* generally opens around this date and runs until Christmas.

December 6 — Saint Nicholas' Day — Fourth Century Bishop of Myra, whose generosity made him the original Santa Claus, comes calling with presents on Saint Nicholas' Eve and his grim assistants may also carry switches for bratty kids. Many fairs open on this day and *Spekulatius* (stamped cinnamon cookies) are passed around quite lavishly.

December 8—Second Sunday of Advent—Friends come calling and join their hosts in prayers and carols as the second Advent candle is lit in Lutheran homes. Catholics light this candle a day earlier. Baked goods are trotted out and consumed without delay.

December 13—Thousands of Nuremberg youngsters carrying lanterns with candles inside march in procession to the city's most prominent castle, where they sing carols and enact a tableau about the Nativity.

December 15—Third Sunday of Advent—Prayers, carols and celebrations as the third Advent candle is lit.

December 21 — Saint Thomas' Day — An especially rich fruitcake is baked and dancing continues far into the night.

December 22—Fourth Advent Sunday—Fourth and final Advent candle is lit.

December 23 — "Eve of the Eve" — The Virgin Mary and flights of angels fly over the land bringing advance word of Christ's birth. Last real working day before Christmas.

December 24—Christmas Eve—Work stops and practically all offices close until December 27. But mother is swamped with baking, present wrapping, tree decorating and children tending. In Westphalia children leave "gimme" notes on windowsills for the Christ Child. He comes and goes undetected, leaving fruits, sweets and presents. As night descends, the tree is lit and the family sings *Stille Nacht* or *O Tannenbaum.* The presents are distributed. In Lorraine the Yule Log is ignited and will burn for three days. In northern Germany there are "Star of Seven" processions with hundreds carrying lighted seven-branch candlesticks as they march through open fields. At *Berchtesgaden* over 1,200 members of holiday shooting clubs climb the mountains wearing ancient costumes and carrying antique firearms. At midnight they will fire many echoing volleys. They'll repeat the sequence on New Year's Eve. Now, it's done for the sheer pleas-

A modern mother and child celebrate the traditional lighting of the Advent Candle.

"…HE COMES AND GOES UNDETECTED, LEAVING FRUITS, SWEETS AND PRESENTS"

"...THE OLD YEAR GOES OUT THE DOOR"

Golden brown and ginger sweet the holiday gingerbread men begin to come to life.

ure of making a thunderous racket; once it was thought to banish evil spirits. Carp is the main dish of the Christmas Eve supper. Many small towns have brass bands to play Christmas tunes. There are pleasure jaunts in brightly-decorated sleighs with Christmas bells jangling. Almost everyone attends midnight church services. The Christ Child in his crib, figures of the Holy Family and carvings of the animals in the Bethlehem stable are displayed under every household Christmas tree. Some of them show superb craftsmanship, exemplifying the essentially religious character of a German Christmas. None of this distracts the

holiday celebrants from consuming an enormous quantity of rich food.

December 25—Christmas Day—Both Catholic and Lutheran families attend daytime church services. In the Austrian Tyrol the Miracle Plays which were once banned by the church are performed. A goose dinner is served. It is primarily a family day with relatives dropping in toward afternoon to view the tree and exchange presents.

December 26—Saint Stephen's Day—He was a patron saint of horsemen and many communities have mounted processions on this day of the three-day "High Christmas" celebration.

December 28—Holy Innocents' Day— Marks the slaughter of children by King Herod. German children presumably square the old account by carrying switches with which they pretend to swat adults and are placated with presents.

Nestled under the tree are several of the delights of a traditional German Christmas.

December 31 — New Year's Eve — Restaurants serve carp. Carp is supposed to be lucky, and the diner who saves a few of its shiny scales may anticipate prosperity in the year ahead. *Sylvesterabend,* a hot, spiced punch, is served with *Pfannkuchen* (doughnuts). In Wuppertal, the favored pastry of the day is *Balbauschen* (fried cake stuffed with raisins and currants). There are early evening church services throughout Germany followed a little later by universal merriment. By custom Lower Rhinelanders play cards until midnight, then everyone throws down his cards and shouts *"Prosit Neujahr!"* (Happy New Year!) In most communities the residents poke their heads out the windows as midnight nears. At the first peal of the New Year bells, there are kisses and New Year's greetings. In a few villages the night watchman pauses to recite this old verse:

> "In the name of the Lord
> The Old Year goes out the door.
> This is my wish for all of you:
> Peace everlasting, and
> Praise to God, our Lord."

January 6 — Epiphany, also known as Twelfth Night or the Festival of the Three Kings — Many high-spirited parties highlight this day. The guest who discovers a bean in his portion of cake becomes King of the Feast and may issue all manner of ridiculous orders. In southern and western Germany, salt and pieces of chalk are consecrated. Salt is for the animals to lick. Chalk is to write the names of

"...NO ONE
IS LEFT OUT"

*A young girl happily marks off the days until
Christmas on the Advent Calendar.*

*Marking the coming of the Christmas season
marksmen sound their guns. Right, a boy
shares Christmas with his horses.*

the Three Kings, Caspar, Melchior and Balthazar, who visited the infant Jesus, and to ask their protection against fire and flood. In Pottenstein, Bavaria, the Procession of Light winds through the town. Bells are rung, bonfires lighted on the mountaintops and the town castle is floodlighted. Star shells are fired and a church service concludes the celebration.

January 13—Octave of Epiphany—Groups of four boys each march in the streets of southern Germany. One carries a lighted star on a pole and the others are dressed as the Three Kings. They may carry a crib to leave with some needy family. Along their way, they sing "Star Songs" and on that note the Christmas season melodiously departs.

No city or region of Germany has a monopoly on Christmas, but perhaps the oldest and most impressive of its public Yuletide observances is the Nuremberg Fair or *Christkindlmarkt*. Nuremberg itself is a bundle of contradictions: nine centuries old, home of the German toy-making industry, quaint and medieval; it is also a highly-sophisticated industrial city of nearly 500,000 people. The old-fashioned side of the city is expressed in the Fair held annually in the Main Market Square. Brightly painted horse-drawn coaches rattle through the streets daily carrying passengers to and from the Fair. It is easy to see why visiting monarchs and their entourages once came from all parts of Europe to view the Nuremberg Fair.

Early in December two trumpeters in medieval costumes and flanked by two angels appear on the gallery of the Church of our Lady which overlooks the square. They are accompanied by a Christ Child figure and invite all to attend the Fair. There is an old tradition that the Christ Child once visited the Fair and delivered presents to the faithful.

Toymakers and woodcarvers produce their finest work for the Fair and only articles directly related to Christmas are sold there.

Among the items you can scarcely overlook are the tinseled "Angel Dolls" sold at many

"…CELEBRATION STARTS AT DAYBREAK"

The trumpeters of Munich herald the season midst the traditional symbols. Left, a wooden angel beckons. Right, St. Nick talks with a German schoolboy.

booths. These have a 300-year history. The first of them was made by a heartbroken father honoring the memory of his beloved, only daughter. There's a happier connotation to the "Little Prune People"—edible dolls with feet, legs and arms of prunes and raisins, a large fig for a body and a walnut for a head. Cookies and cakes formed into animals, dwarfs, stars and other shapes share the food booths with *Kringel,* semi-transparent cookies in figure-eight shape so that they can be hung on a Christmas tree. *Lubecker Marzipan* is a candy that imitates fruit and vegetables so closely that first time viewers are often fooled. Tidbits such as roast sausage, grilled herring, hard spicy peppermint and frosted cookies blend with other fragrant foods to produce an intoxicating aroma. It is no place for a picky eater.

For most modern German families who keep Christmas in the traditional manner, the celebration starts at daybreak on December 24. The children are shoved out of the house to play or go caroling in the neighborhood. Back in the house, the room where the Christmas tree, secretly stolen into the house a few nights before, stands is locked to all but Mother who traditionally decorates the tree by herself. If she is very traditional, she clips wax candles on first. Then gilded nuts and red apples. Candies wrapped in fancy tinsel paper twinkle from deep within the boughs. Then the magnificent hand-blown glass ornaments which have been passed down for generations are hung. Paper chains and angel hair add their special magic. Then the special cookies mother has been baking for weeks especially for the tree and the *Springerle,* each with a special Yuletide symbol or figure on it, are placed on the tree. To finish off the tree she puts on gingerbread figures and cookies.

Holiday decorations light up the streets of Cologne as a family, right, enjoys one of the many feasts of Christmas.

At the base of the tree goes the Creche, usually a family heirloom of figures in porcelain or wood carved hundreds of years ago. And then the presents go nearby the tree next to a figure of the *Christkind* (Christ Child) dressed in white robes wearing a crown of gold.

The entire room takes on the air of a fantasy —with *Lebkuchen* (honey cakes) and gingerbread houses and prune people everywhere. And the smells which have filled the house for weeks—the cinnamon, the cloves, the vanilla and the ginger—mingle with the aroma of the fir tree to mix an even more magical air and heighten the excitement.

At six PM, to the sound of tinkling bells, the doors are thrown open and the family is invited in to view the tree for the first time. Before the presents are opened, father reads the story of the birth of Christ. Then, after much ripping and tearing at paper, all the presents are opened and the time for Christmas Eve dinner has finally arrived.

As the family gathers around the table to enjoy a feast of *Karpfen* (carp, a traditional favorite) and butter, whipped cream and horseradish, special red cabbage with bacon, they retell again the miracle of the coming of Christ. When dessert arrives, usually a specially decorated honey cake or *Stollen* pastry, the children begin to sing carols.

"…THE ENTIRE ROOM TAKES ON THE AIR OF A FANTASY"

"...GERMANY AND CHRISTMAS WERE MADE FOR EACH OTHER"

After dinner comes the high point of Christmas Eve when the whole family goes to the midnight service.

With the coming of dawn and Christmas Day itself, everyone looks forward to the *Grosses Weihnachtses,* the Big Christmas Feast. Even though no one wants to spoil their appetites, there are plenty of *Naschen* everywhere. One of the specialties is a chocolate pretzel called a *Brezel.*

Also, there are the ever-lasting cookies called *Dauergebach.* Mother began preparing them way back in July. They come in all shapes, sizes, colors, flavors and designs. Everything from stars to angels and even symbolic *Pelznickel,* one of the legendary fur covered creatures that terrorizes bad little German children.

According to ancient customs, there are always bowls of apples, fruits and nuts as well. *Apfel, Nuss* and *Mandelkern,* as an old children's rhyme tells, are the foods of Christmas. The apple, so the legend goes, stands for the Tree of Knowledge in Paradise. Nuts remind one of the difficulties and mysteries of life. And the fruits recall the bounty that is Christmas.

But, incredibly, the real feast of Christmas is yet to come. That takes place at midday on Christmas Day. And what a great meal it is. By tradition, it was literally a feast to be set before a king—symbolically the Christ Child. At such a dinner one would sit down to a roast hare or plump goose stuffed with apples, plums, chestnuts, and onions plus a variety of salads, ranging from red beets to spiced cabbage. Of course, there's always wine to toast the season and vegetables specially made for the Christmas feast.

And for those who can stand it, there is another round of desserts. Everything from a *Frankfurter Kranz*—a round cake stuffed with hazel nuts and almonds—to *Pfeffernusse,* to *Dresdner Stollen,* the traditional Christmas fruit bread that gets better as it ages.

The season of Christmas seems to make everyone more conscious of the past and all the traditions which have built up over the centuries. Christmas celebrations are truly festivals of togetherness. A time when friends, neighbors and relatives get together to retell and celebrate a miracle that happened almost two thousand years ago.

Which was invented first—the picture-book landscape of Germany in mid-winter with its evergreen forests, snow-covered mountains and crystal-clear, starry nights—or the fun, feeding and piety of a real German Christmas? There is probably no reasonable answer to this question, but the two elements came together hundreds of years ago: Germany and Christmas were made for each other.

Under a blanket of snow the town of Mittenwald awaits Christmas, just as it always has, which would have made these children of long ago feel right at home.

O
TANNENBAUM

Whatever legend you happen to believe, whatever was the true story of how the Christmas tree came into being, the tree has become one of the most beautiful symbols of the Christmas season. Decorated with all sorts of whimsical delights, ornaments handed down through the generations, hundreds of tiny lights, gingerbread figures, gilded fruits and nuts, each tree takes on a personality of its own.

Throughout Germany, the aroma of fir boughs fills every room during the Christmas

season. And every home has a tree. In a traditional home, the tree, secreted into the house just a few days before Christmas, is decorated on Christmas Eve. Then the whole family gathers around the tree, exchanging gifts and singing carols. Because the trees are so very fancifully decorated, many modern German families put them up soon after the beginning of the Christmas season so that everyone can enjoy them for a few extra days.

Whenever the tree appears in a German home, it is certain to bring delight and excitement to everyone filling the house with its scent, adding to all the merriment of the season and reminding everyone of the miracle that happened almost two thousand years ago.

A CHRISTMAS CARNIVAL

Approximately three weeks before Christmas Day, the *Christkindlmarkt* (Christ Child market) opens.

The most opulent and most widely known of these is held in Nuremberg. The fair is set up in the oldest section of the city, the *Altstat*. Heavily damaged in World War II, it has been completely restored to its medieval splendor. As a result, visitors have the feeling they are visiting a fair that hasn't changed very much in centuries.

Other *Christkindlmarkts* are held throughout Germany—in Munich, Hamburg, Bremen and Frankfort. Customs may vary throughout the countryside, but all the *Christkindlmarkts* share one thing in common: only Christmas goodies, toys and ornaments are sold here.

In Nuremberg, the fair itself is set up in the center of the square in front of one of the oldest churches in the city. In the middle of all the booths stands an enormous Creche. Almost life-size figures of the Three Kings, the Virgin Mary, Joseph, farm animals and angels watch over the Christ Child crib. Many of the figures were commissioned by the local nobility especially for the fair almost 400 years ago.

In the booths surrounding the Creche, traditional folk crafts are displayed. Some booths specialize in prune people, the whimsical fig and raisin dolls dressed in assorted native costumes. Others sell hand blown glass ornaments made the same way they were hundreds of years ago. Still others sell all sorts of Christmas cookies, everything from gingerbread people to chocolate *Brezels,* to *Kringel,* the semi-transparent figure-eight cookies that are hung on the tree.

The Christkindlmarkt opens in Munich.

Other booths at the *Christkindlmarkt* virtually burst with all kinds of foods—grilled herring, roast sausage, spicy peppermints, sugar scrolls and Marizpan. Each booth with all its foodstuffs is more tempting than the next.

Children love the many booths filled with toys. Here you will find toy soldiers and dolls of all shapes and kinds made today the same way German craftsmen made them long ago.

Ablaze with lights, the Christkindlmarkt in Nuremberg invites everyone to enjoy the Christmas season.

The opening day of the *Christkindlmarkt* is a very special one. City officials give speeches and the Christ Child (usually one of the city officials) dressed in white silk robes with golden wings blesses the fair and all who come to it with a special poem. The Christ Child then leads the way into the fair and it is officially open.

Yet another beautiful pageant takes place at the *Christkindlmarkt* in Nuremberg. On December 13th, the children dressed in white

robes assemble near the Creche at sundown, each carrying a homemade lantern with a lighted candle inside. Slowly they make their way through the streets, singing carols as they go, until they reach the castle high above the city. Here they present a medieval tableau, retelling the miracle of Christ's birth.

The *Christkindlmarkt* is truly a dream come true. A massive fair completely dedicated to the merriment of the Christmas season. A tradition Germany is most proud of, and one that will probably continue for centuries to come. One glance tells you why monarchs and their entourages came from all over Europe to join in the merriment, filling the air with the sounds of their horse drawn coaches. And one glance tells you why people today are irresistably drawn to the *Christkindlmarkt*. Some things never change.

Everyone who comes to the Christkindlmarkt catches the Christmas spirit as they see the Creche and stalls loaded with goodies.

MAKE A JOYFUL NOISE

Caroling is one of the oldest and most beautiful of all Christmas customs. Walking softly through the snow, strolling bands of singers carry the sounds of Christmas across the land.

Carols originally were folk melodies. Sung in an attempt to bring the miracle of Christ's birth to all the people, they date from the days of the earliest Christians.

Popular throughout every country the carol, as we know it today, was first developed in Germany.

One of the earliest known carols is associated with the life of the saint, King Wenceslas. Ruler of Bohemia in the 10th century, the carol *Good King Wenceslas* tells all men to treat each other as brothers.

The idea for yet another kind of carol was developed in the 12th century by Saint Francis, who wondered how to bring the message of God to the people in a way they could understand. To do this, he dramatized the story of Christ's birth and glorified the crib scene. This crib became the focal point for several carols. The most famous of these, is *Away in a Manger,* written in the 15th century.

Martin Luther was, perhaps the foremost influence upon carols. Realizing early in life that music was most important, he considered it "a gift of God."

According to legend, Luther wrote one of the most famous carols while rocking his young son's crib one Christmas Eve. Taking an old German folk song as his guide, he composed all 15 verses of *From Heaven Above.* To this day, the carol is sung from the dome of the Kreuz Church in Dresden shortly before daybreak on Christmas morning.

In 1597 one of the most majestic of all Christmas carols was written. Philipp Nicolai, pastor of the church at Unna, sat reflecting on the fact that many of his parishoners had been felled by plagues. Slowly, as if to bathe his sorrows, the words of *How Brightly Beams The Morning Star* came to him. First published in 1599, it was later used by Johann Sebastian Bach as a basis for one of his preludes.

Another favorite German carol is *Hark! The Herald Angels Sing.* Written by an Irishman, Charles Wesley, in 1739, it wasn't until Felix Mendelssohn composed a new melody for it, in 1840, that the carol became popular.

The custom of a Christmas tree is a very old one dating from the days of the early Romans and their festival of *Saturnalia.* A series of barbarian invasions brought the custom back to Germany, but it wasn't unitl the time of Martin Luther that the tree and all that surrounds it became part of the Christmas tradition.

To glorify the tree and the Christmas season, the carol *O Tannenbaum* was written. This carol has become one of the most widely sung carols in the world and a symbol itself of all that has come to mean Christmas.

Hark! the Herald Angels Sing

CHARLES WESLEY, 1739

FELIX MENDELSSOHN, 1840
Arr. by W.H. Cummings, 1855

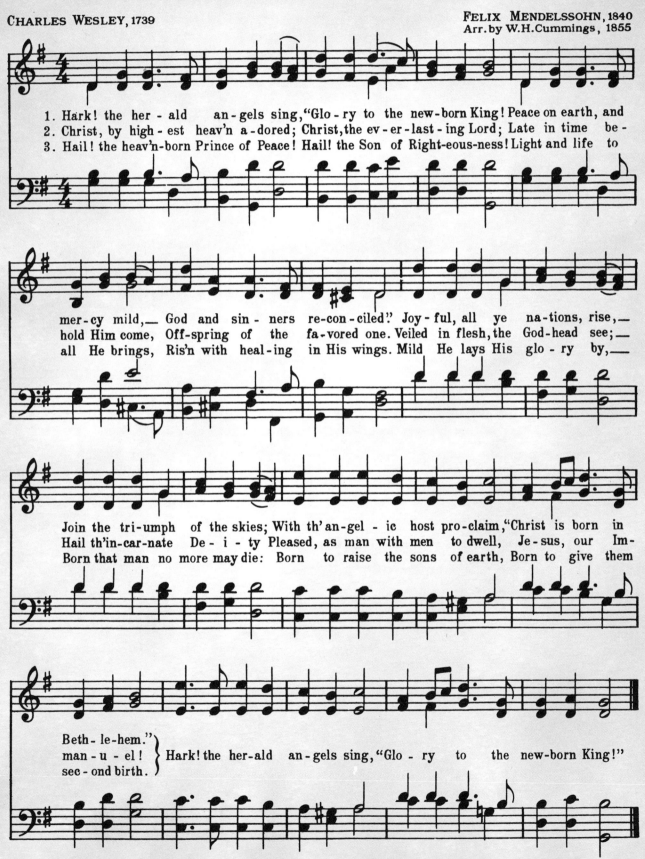

1. Hark! the her - ald an - gels sing, "Glo - ry to the new-born King! Peace on earth, and
2. Christ, by high - est heav'n a - dored; Christ, the ev - er - last - ing Lord; Late in time be -
3. Hail! the heav'n-born Prince of Peace! Hail! the Son of Right-eous-ness! Light and life to

mer - cy mild,— God and sin - ners re-con - ciled." Joy - ful, all ye na-tions, rise,—
hold Him come, Off - spring of the fa-vored one. Veiled in flesh, the God-head see;—
all He brings, Ris'n with heal - ing in His wings. Mild He lays His glo - ry by,—

Join the tri - umph of the skies; With th'an-gel - ic host pro-claim, "Christ is born in
Hail th'in-car-nate De - i - ty Pleased, as man with men to dwell, Je - sus, our Im-
Born that man no more may die: Born to raise the sons of earth, Born to give them

Beth - le-hem."
man - u - el! } Hark! the her-ald an - gels sing, "Glo - ry to the new-born King!"
sec - ond birth.

From Heaven Above
(Vom Himmel hoch)

MARTIN LUTHER, 1535
Translated by Catherine Winkworth

Melody from SCHUMANN'S Hymn Book, 1539
Arranged by Johann Sebastian Bach

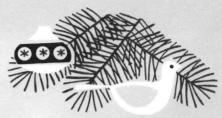

Larghetto

1. From heav'n a-bove to earth I come ___ To bear good news to ev'ry home; ___ Glad ti-dings of great joy ___ I bring, ___ Where-of I now will say and sing. ___

2. To you this night is born a child ___ Of Ma-ry, cho-sen moth-er mild; ___ This lit-tle child, of low-ly birth, ___ Shall be the joy of all the earth. ___

3. Glo-ry to God in high-est heav'n, ___ Who un-to man His Son hath given! ___ While an-gels sing with pi-ous mirth ___ A glad New Year to all the earth. ___

The Original German

1. Vom Himmel hoch, da komm ich her,
Ich bring' euch gute neue Mär.
Der guten Mär bring ich so viel,
Davon ich sing'n und sagen will.

2. Euch ist ein Kindlein heut gebor'n,
Von einer Jungfrau auserkorn,
Ein Kindlein so zart und fein,
Das soll eur Freud' und Wonne sein.

3. Lob, Ehr' sei Gott im höchsten Thron,
Der uns schenkt seinen ein'gen Sohn,
Des freuen sich der Engel Schar
Und singen uns solch neues Jahr.

Good King Wenceslas

(Story on page 64)

John Mason Neal

TRADITIONAL
Arr. by Sir John Stainer

Moderato

CHO. 1. Good King Wen-ces-las look'd out On the Feast of Steph-en,
TEN. S. 2. "Hith-er, page, and stand by me, If thou know'st it, tell-ing;
TEN. S. 3. "Bring me flesh, and bring me wine, Bring me pine-logs hith-er;

When the snow lay round a-bout, Deep and crisp and e-ven;
Yon-der peas-ant, who is he? Where, and what his dwell-ing?"
Thou and I will see him dine When we bear them thith-er."

Bright-ly shone the moon that night, Tho' the frost was cru-el,
SOP. S. "Sire, he lives a good league hence, Un-der-neath the moun-tain;
CHO. Page and mon-arch forth they went, Forth they went to-geth-er;

poco piu lento

When a poor man came in sight, Gath-'ring win-ter fu-el.
Right a-gainst the for-est fence, By Saint Ag-nes' foun-tain."
Thro' the rude wind's wild la-ment And the bit-ter weath-er.

SOP. S. 4. "Sire, the night is darker now,
And the wind blows stronger;
Fails my heart, I know not how,
I can go no longer."

TEN. S. "Mark my footsteps, my good page,
Tread thou in them boldly:
Thou shalt find the winter's rage
Freeze thy blood less coldly."

CHO. 5. In his master's steps he trod,
Where the snow lay dinted;
Heat was in the very sod
Which the saint had printed;
Therefore, Christian men, be sure,
Wealth or rank possessing,
Ye who now will bless the poor,
Shall yourselves find blessing.

Away in a Manger

CRADLE HYMN
(Boys' Voices)

15th CENTURY GERMAN

GERMAN MELODY
Arr. by T.O.K.

Dolce

1. A - way in a man - ger no crib for a bed, The lit - tle Lord
2. The cat - tle are low - ing, the poor ba - by wakes, But lit - tle Lord
3. Be near me, Lord Je - sus, I ask Thee to stay Close by me for -

Je - sus laid down His sweet head, The stars in the sky, ____ looked
Je - sus, no cry - ing He makes, I love Thee, Lord Je - sus, look
ev - er, and love me, I pray; Bless all the dear chil - dren in

down where He lay, The lit - tle Lord Je - sus, a - sleep on the hay.
down from the sky, And stay by my cra - dle, till morn - ing is nigh.
Thy ten - der care, And take us to heav - en, to live with Thee there.

O Christmas Tree
(O Tannenbaum)

English Version by
T. O. K. and F. F.

GERMAN FOLK SONG

Moderately

1. O Christ - mas Tree, O Christ - mas Tree, For - ev - er true your
2. O Christ - mas Tree, O Christ - mas Tree, You fill my heart with
3. O Christ - mas Tree, O Christ - mas Tree, How bright - ly shine thy
4. O Christ - mas Tree, O Christ - mas Tree, How stur - dy God hath

col - or! Your boughs so green in sum - mer time, Stay
mu - sic. Re - mind - ing me on Christ - mas day, To
can - dles! And from each bough a ti - ny light Adds
made thee! Thou bidst us all place faith - ful - ly Our

brave - ly green in win - ter time, O Christ - mas Tree, O
think of you and then be gay. O Christ - mas Tree, O
to the splen - dor of the sight. O Christ - mas Tree, O
trust in God un - chang - ing - ly. O Christ - mas Tree, O

Christ - mas Tree, For - ev - er true your col - or.
Christ - mas Tree, You fill my heart with mus - ic.
Christ - mas Tree, How bright - ly shine thy can - dles!
Christ - mas Tree, How stur - dy God hath made thee!

Silent Night
(*Stille Nacht*)

JOSEPH MÖHR, 1818   FRANZ GRÜBER, 1818

1. Si - lent night! Ho - ly night! All is calm, all is bright.
2. Si - lent night! Ho - ly night! Shep - herds quake at the sight!
3. Si - lent night! Ho - ly night! Son of God, love's pure light!

'Round yon vir - gin moth - er and child!   Ho - ly In - fant, so ten - der and mild,
Glo - ries stream from heav - en a - far,   Heav'n - ly hosts sing, "Al - le - lu - ia!"
Ra - diant beams from Thy ho - ly face   With the dawn of re - deem - ing grace,

Sleep in heav - en - ly peace, ——   Sleep in heav - en - ly peace. ——
Christ, the Sav - ior, is born! ——   Christ, the Sav - ior, is born! ——
Je - sus, Lord, at Thy birth, ——   Je - sus, Lord, at Thy birth. ——

German Version

1. Stille Nacht, heilige Nacht!
 Alles schläft, einsam wacht
 Nur das traute, hoch heilige Paar.
 Holder Knabe im lockigen Haar,
 Schlaf in himmlischer Ruh!
 Schlaf in himmlischer Ruh!

2. Stille Nacht, heilige Nacht!
 Hirten erst kund gemacht
 Durch der Engel Halleluja!
 Tönt es laut von fern und nah:
 Christ, der Retter, ist da!
 Christ, der Retter, ist da!

3. Stille Nacht, heilige Nacht!
 Gottes Sohn, O wie lacht
 Lieb' aus deinem göttlichen Mund,
 Da uns schlägt die rettende Stund',
 Christ, in deiner Geburt!
 Christ, in deiner Geburt!

"...THE WORK
OF SOME VERY HUNGRY
MICE"

Had it not been for the work of some very hungry mice one cold Christmas Eve long ago, the world's most widely sung carol, *Silent Night,* might never have been written.

In the town of Oberstdorf, Bavaria, on Christmas Eve, 1818, Franz Gruber, the organist at Saint Nicholas Church discovered that mice had eaten away at the bellows of the organ and ruined it.

He had to find a way to have music on Christmas Day, so he suggested to Joseph Mohr, the Vicar of the church, that perhaps a new song could be written that would carry them through this emergency.

Accordingly, Mohr wrote some verses beginning with the words, *Stille Nacht,* while Gruber hastily composed a melody. Within a few hours they sang their new song at the Christmas Midnight Mass to the entire congregation, accompanied only by a guitar.

Over time, the origin of the carol became lost. It was thought to be an old folk song that had been passed around the countryside for many years. And it wasn't until an inquiry was made by the musicians of the royal court in Berlin in 1854, that the true origin of the carol came to light. Today, *Silent Night* is sung the world over, in more than 90 different languages.

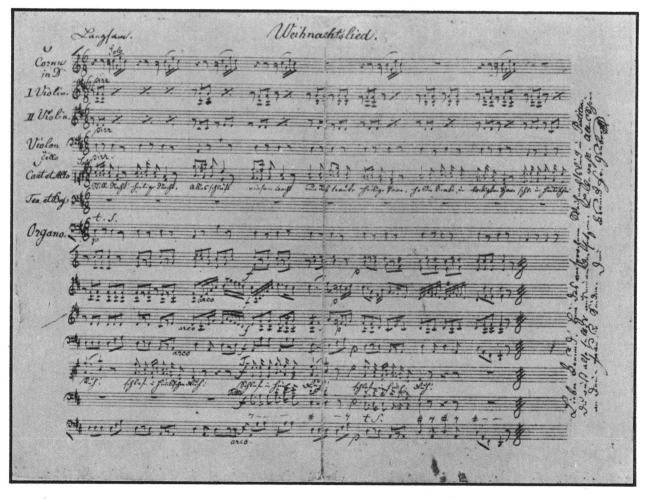

PRUNE PEOPLE AND GINGERBREAD HOUSES

Among the most fanciful of all the delights of Christmas in Germany are the Prune People and the Gingerbread Houses.

Sold by the thousands at the *Christkindlmarkt* in every major city, Prune People are truly delightful whimsies. No one knows where they originated. They simply seem to have arrived on the scene. Considered a true folk art craft, they are a veritable nation of little creatures.

Prune People come in all shapes and sizes. Each is unique: hand painted faces with very wise expressions, faces bubbling over with laughter, faces with looks of astonishment, crafty-eyed faces that appear ready to pounce at you at a moment's notice—all attached to bodies clothed in costumes of every shape, color, description and size.

A great deal of thought goes into the making of these Prune People. Because each one is unique and so many thousands of them are sold at the *Christkindlmarkts,* craftsmen begin making them way back in July. By early November their studios are cluttered with armies of Prune People.

Made from raisins, figs, walnuts, prunes and peanuts, the Prune People add a special merriment of their own to the holiday season. And every child longs to have at least one Prune Person for his or her very own each Christmas.

How Gingerbread Houses became one of the rituals of a German Christmas is another mystery. All we know is that for hundreds of years these extremely ornate and imaginative creations have appeared, often as if by magic, at Christmastime in every home.

A children's fantasy or an adult playtoy, *Lebkuchen Hauschen,* as they are known in German, are not exceptionally difficult to make at home. And once they are assembled, they take on a magic all their own and lend it to the Christmas festivities.

Gingerbread Houses come in all sizes and shapes. Some have gingerbread Christmas trees on the lawn in front of them. Others have sleighs loaded down with Christmas gifts, racing off to who knows where in the snow. While others are absolute monster houses, decorated with every conceivable kind of Christmas cookie and decoration.

With any luck, you can make a Gingerbread House of your very own at home. In theory these houses are permanent creations, but with the enticing smell of ginger filling the air, don't expect it to last much longer than a few weeks. Children have been known to devour entire Gingerbread Houses at a single sitting.

This Christmas, try adding some Prune People and a Gingerbread House to your Christmas festivities. And help carry on a tradition, hundreds of years old, that helps make Christmas so very special.

A GERMAN FEAST IN AMERICA

A DINNER
THAT CAN GO ON
FOREVER

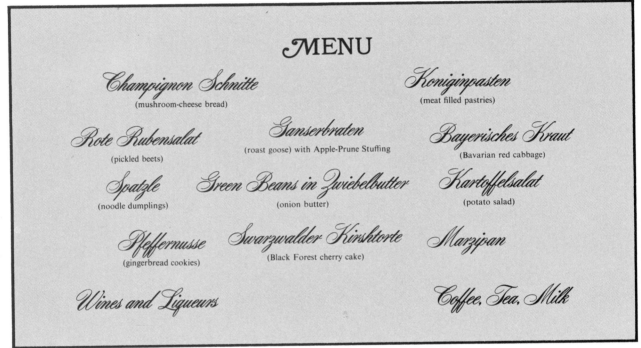

MENU

Champignon Schnitte
(mushroom-cheese bread)

Koniginpasten
(meat filled pastries)

Rote Rubensalat
(pickled beets)

Ganserbraten
(roast goose) with Apple-Prune Stuffing

Bayerisches Kraut
(Bavarian red cabbage)

Spatzle
(noodle dumplings)

Green Beans in Zwiebelbutter
(onion butter)

Kartoffelsalat
(potato salad)

Pfeffernusse
(gingerbread cookies)

Swarzwalder Kirshtorte
(Black Forest cherry cake)

Marzipan

Wines and Liqueurs

Coffee, Tea, Milk

For days you've been polishing your best silver and cleaning all your holiday china. The house has been filled with the aroma of so many Christmas treats for so long it seems difficult to believe the actual Christmas Day Feast is finally here.

Bringing a traditional German Christmas dinner like the one pictured on the preceding pages is actually fairly simple—if creating any large holiday dinner can be called simple. Many of these foods that have now become the staples of our Christmas dinner are actually of German origin brought here by the many thousands of German people who immigrated to America over the past two centuries. We are not suggesting you attempt to serve your family a whole roast boar for Christmas any more than you should try to re-create the entire display of Christmas cookies opposite. But it is not all that difficult to serve up a roast goose

dinner with all the German-style trimmings.

The recipes included on the recipe cards are not difficult, although some of them do require a little more time and effort than others. We have chosen those dishes found in a traditional German Christmas Feast whose ingredients can be purchased easily no matter where you live. They are all authentic dishes adapted for American kitchens.

Starting with an abundance of appetizers the dinner continues on for several courses—roast goose plump with apple-prune stuffing, a variety of salads, vegetables, and a series of desserts beginning with Black Forest cherry cake, marzipan and gingerbread cookies.

And if that doesn't sound like enough, there are always the traditional wines to toast everyone's health and wish them well in the coming year. Truly a feast to set before a king. And one your family will always remember.

CHRISTMAS IS SOMETHING TO MAKE AT HOME

Christmas just seems to be more festive when there are things to do and projects for everyone in the family to help make. In Germany this has been a tradition passed down through the centuries. Long before the actual Christmas season, entire families are hard at work making ornaments to hang on the tree.

To help you give a German flavor to your tree we have developed this series of projects. Most of the materials you will need can be easily obtained. Several of them are so simple that even the smallest children can participate.

SPIKEY CHRISTMAS STARS

Once you get the knack, these are quite easy to make. It is best to use a silver or gold foil paper that will take a curl.

1. Cut a circle 6 inches in diameter from foil.

2. Mark off eight equal sections, being careful not to draw a line to the center of the circle. Leave a circle about 1½ inches in diameter in the center.

3. Cut along each of the fold lines.

4. With the tip of a sharp pencil, start folding the edges of each cut section in a clockwise fashion (see diagram). Continue roll-ing each section until the piece takes on the shape of a cone.

5. Cut several more of these circles, follow-ing steps 1 through 4.

6. Put one layer on top of the first so that the points of one circle fall in the open spaces of the layer below.

7. Continue placing each layer upon layer, glueing the centers together until you have formed a half ball. The more layers you place on top of one another, the fuller the ornament will appear. Then make a sec-ond half ball and glue both halves together.

8. Hang from tree with transparent thread.

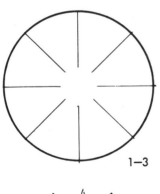

1–3

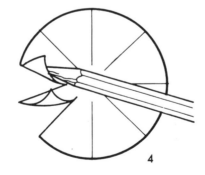

4

4

5–6

PLEATED STARS

This is another variation of the symbolic star. It is most effective when made from gold or silver heavyweight paper or foil. But it can be made from excess wrapping paper.

1. Cut a strip of paper 10¼ inches by 3 inches.

2. Mark off 1 inch sections on this strip, noting that there will be a ¼ inch overlap at the end of the strip.

3. Carefully fold along the lines you have drawn.

4. Now, with the paper held tightly folded, draw cutting lines as shown in the diagram.

Draw diagonally from the top corner to a point opposite which is 1 inch from the bottom of the fold. Draw a triangular notch on the fold. (See diagram.)

5. Cut on drawn lines, through all the pleats, being careful to leave that 1 inch area uncut.

6. Glue the ¼ inch piece to the other end of the strip.

7. Open up the star by pulling out the points of the star.

8. Cut another color circle 1½ inch in diameter and glue it to the back of the star at the corner. Attach a string for hanging.

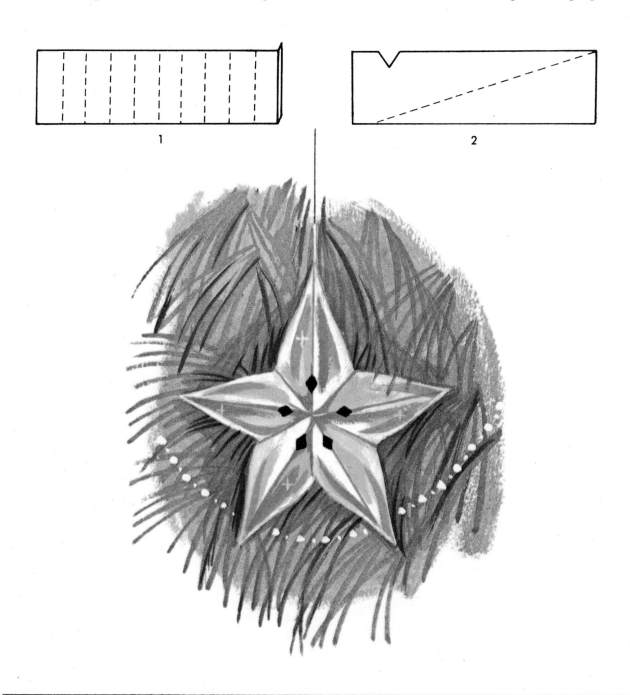

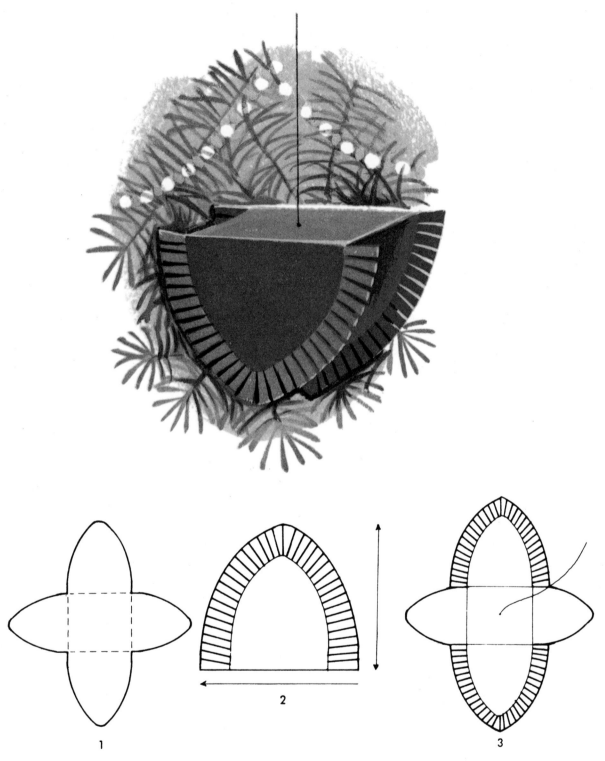

1

2

3

FRINGED BELL

Another of the whimsical bells that help make a Christmas tree what it has come to be —a cornucopia of intricate and beautiful ornaments and lights.

1. You will need construction paper in two colors.

2. Cut one pattern of A (to size) and two of B (to size).

3. Fringe the edges of B by making small slits and glue to the two largest flaps of A. Glue on the underside so that the fringe edges the bell.

4. Fold all flaps down on dotted lines.

5. With needle and thread put a string for hanging through the center.

6. Staple or glue the smaller flaps together at the lowest point.

MODERN BELL

Made from folded and creased gilt paper, these modern bells add a distinctive note to the tree. Unlike ornaments you buy in a store, they uniquely reflect your personal feelings about the holiday.

1. You will need a square of construction paper 5¼ by 5¾ inches for each bell. In addition you will also need gummed stars, glass beads and glitter.

2. Always remember to crease the paper on the same side and unfold it to a square after each step.

3. Fold paper diagonally and crease sharply from corner to corner. Unfold. Crease and fold diagonally from the other two corners. Unfold. (See diagram.)

4. Fold straight across the center, dividing the paper in half. Unfold. Crease in half from the other direction.

5. Open paper to the original square. From one corner bring the edge to the diagonal line and fold. Bring the opposite edge to the same diagonal line and crease. Now the paper looks like a kite.

6. Make "kites" in each corner of the square, following the method described in step 5. This means 8 new lines and the open paper will have this pattern, (see step 6 on diagram.)

7. Push in at the center of each edge. This forms a four-pointed star. Pull the points of the star together to form the bell and push out the center.

8. Knot a thread and sew two gummed stars and two glass beads to the center point. Fasten to it the bell. Bring the points of the star together and sew, leaving enough thread for hanging the bell on the tree.

9. Decorate with glitter.

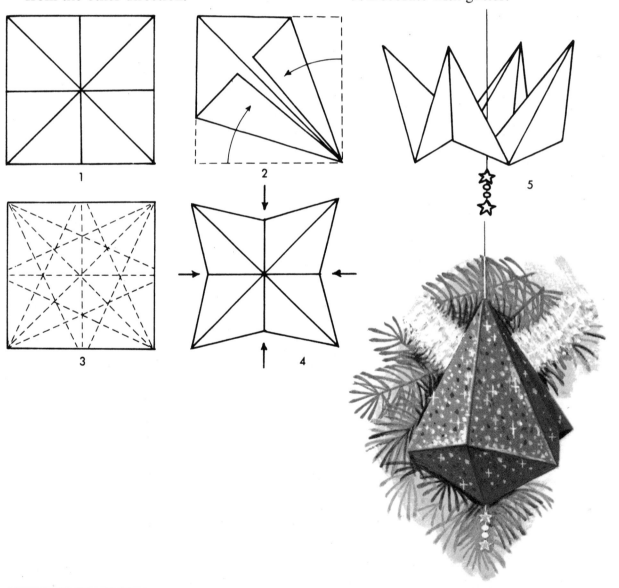

DOVE OF PEACE

Throughout time the dove has meant Peace. This easy-to-make dove is one youngsters as well as adults will have fun making.

1. On heavyweight construction paper trace one dove body, two crowns, two wings and two body strips.

2. Crease the wings and the body strips according to the folds you find on each of the pattern pieces.

3. Glue the pieces to each side of the body with household cement.

4. String from the tree with some thin gold cord.

TRADITIONAL BELL

The bell is a traditional tree ornament, whose heritage goes back to the Sixth Century when Christendom first became fascinated with them. This most traditional of all bells is the simplest of ornaments to make. It looks most spectacular when you construct it out of silver, white and gold paper.

1. Cut out several of the bell pieces from each color paper. (See diagram for shape.)

2. Fold them along the center line.

3. Staple or glue the many different bell pieces together at this center point.

4. Attach a gold cord from the top of the bell for hanging on the tree.

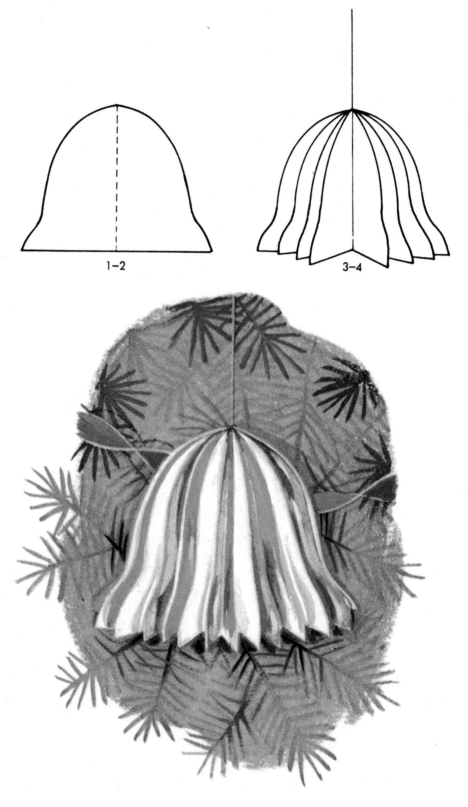

1–2

3–4

RIBBON STAR

Symbolic of the star that led the Three Wise Kings to the Manger where the Christ Child lay, this ornament may appear difficult but is actually quite simple to make. Use a ribbon which is pliable and easy to work. Some are very stiff and won't work in stars.

1. Take four pieces of ribbon, either all the same color or two different colors. Each piece should be ¾ by 24 inches long. Interlock the pieces so they form a basketweave pattern and pull each piece so they come together tightly. (See step 1 in diagram.)

2. Lift the top ribbon pieces together and form a second basketweave.

3. Again, pull the ends together tightly.

4. Bring up one of the loose ends and slip it through one of the open sides, turning the loop inside out with your fingers. (Step 4.)

5. Pull the end through until it forms a point or triangle when you fold it. Repeat with each of the remaining loose ends.

6. Turn the star over and repeat steps 4 and 5 so that you now have eight star points.

7. To make the center star points, lift and fold back one of the top strips. Take a second strip going in the opposite direction (at a 90° angle) and keeping it right side up, loop the strip counterclockwise and slip it under the slot under the raised ribbon (see diagram). Pull through to make a center point.

8. Repeat the same step to form four standing points. To make center points on the opposite side of the star, repeat steps 6 and 7 on the opposite side.

9. Trim excess ribbon and attach to the tree with a loop of thread.

THE HERITAGE OF THE GERMAN ARTIST

Christmas themes have always played a major role in the German artistic heritage. From the massive paintings of the Nativity Scene by famous artists to the simple wood carvings of nameless craftsmen, each creation has tried to capture some part of the spirit of the season. On the following pages are examples of four centuries of German Christmas artistry.

Devoutly religious, German artisans spend months creating the designs, sculptures and paintings which depict the miracle of Christ's birth.

The adoration of the Magi and the journey of the Three Kings have for centuries provided
one of the most bountiful expressions of German artistic craftsmanship.
Because the craftsman often had little information about how the characters should appear to be historically correct,
he clothed his creations as he thought they should look.

*Characteristic of the artistic style of the time, this Adoration of the Shepherds, by
Christian Wilhelm Ernst Dietrich (1712-1774), mixed biblical costumes with those worn by peasants
in the 18th Century and helped make the contemporary viewer feel part of the scene.*

INDEX

ILLUSTRATION ACKNOWLEDGEMENTS:

Cover:	Chicago Museum of Science & Industry
3-5:	E. Lessing
6:	D. Bartcky
8-9:	Staatsbibliothek
11-12:	The Bettmann Archive Inc.
13:	German Infomation Center
14:	E. Bauer
15:	A. Hubrich
16:	(left) C. Teubner; (right) G. Togel
17:	T. Hopker
18:	(left) E. Hartrick; (right) E. Baumann
19:	E. Bauer
20:	D. Bartcky
21:	(left) Bavaria-Verlag; (right) W. Eberhardt
22:	H. Lanks
23:	H. Adam
24:	Staatsbibliothek
25:	Shostal Associates Inc.
26:	German Information Center
27:	S. Bohnacker
28:	C. Anger
29:	(upper left) N. Amann; (upper right) Kosel; (bottom) Staatsbibliothek
31:	P. Kornetzki
32:	Shostal Associates Inc.
33:	(top) Shostal Associates Inc.; (bottom) S. Bohnacker
34:	German National Tourist Office
41:	Staatsbibliothek
42:	W. Bahnmuller
43:	Shostal Associates Inc.
44-45:	Westgate Graphics
47:	N. Amann
49:	P. Keetman
56:	(upper left & right) E. Bauer; (lower left) W. Bahnmuller; (lower right) Pierpont Morgan Library
57:	Shostal Associates Inc.
58:	(clockwise from bottom) H. Arnold; German Information Center; Lauterwasser; German National Tourist Office
59-60-61:	Metropolitan Museum of Art